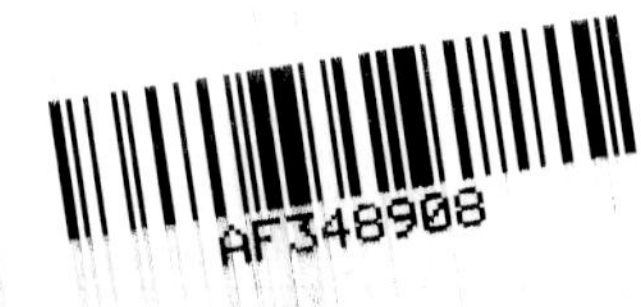

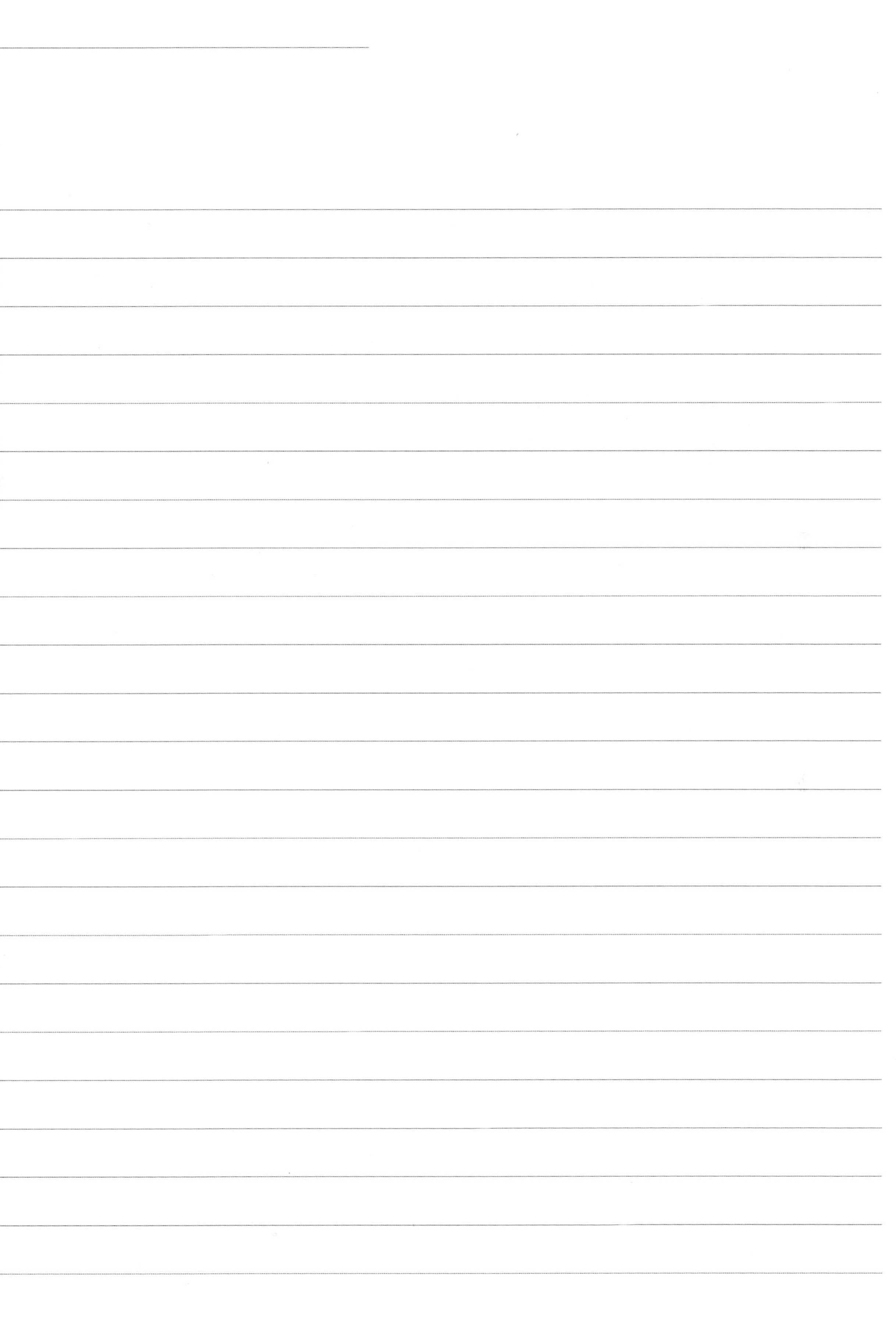

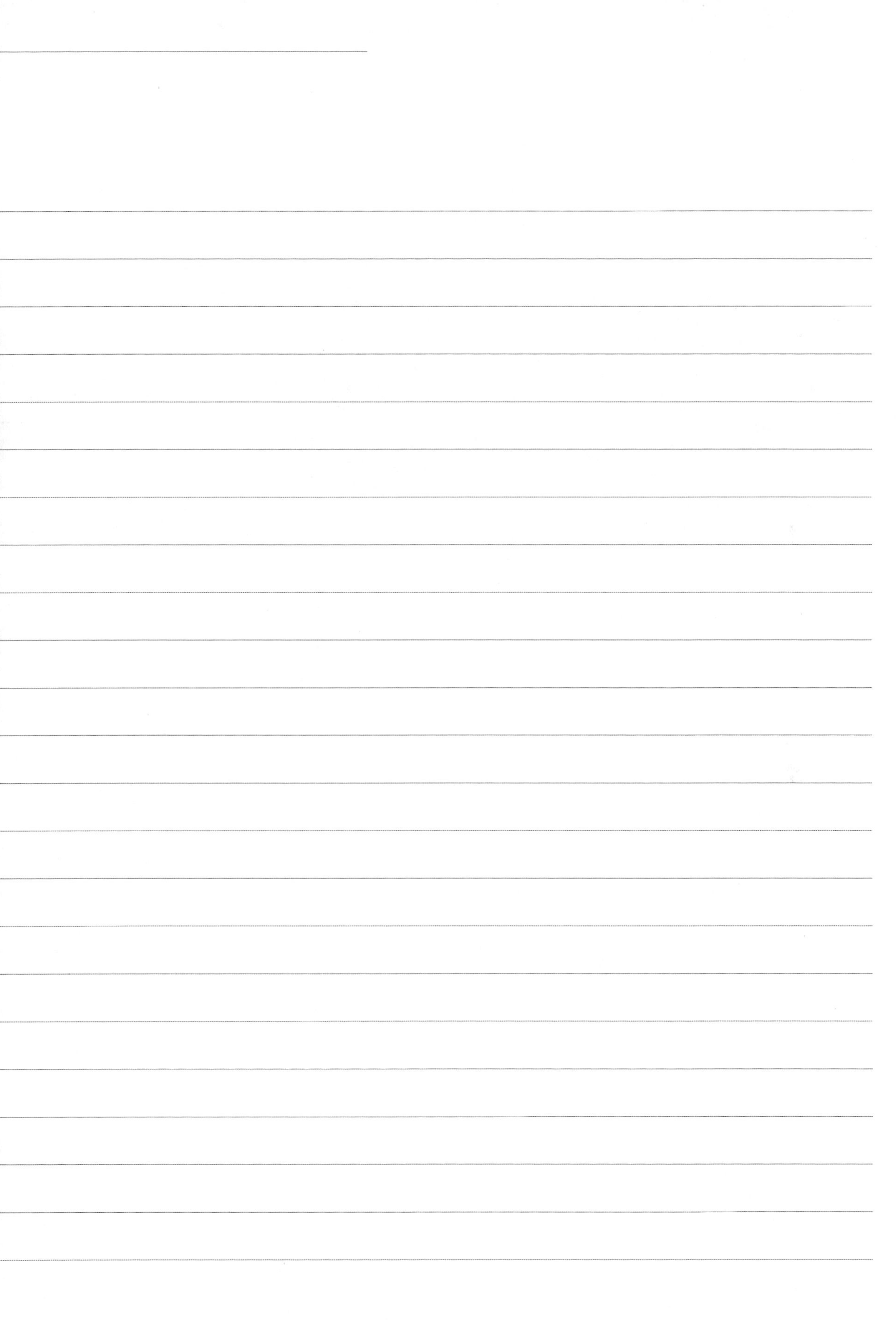

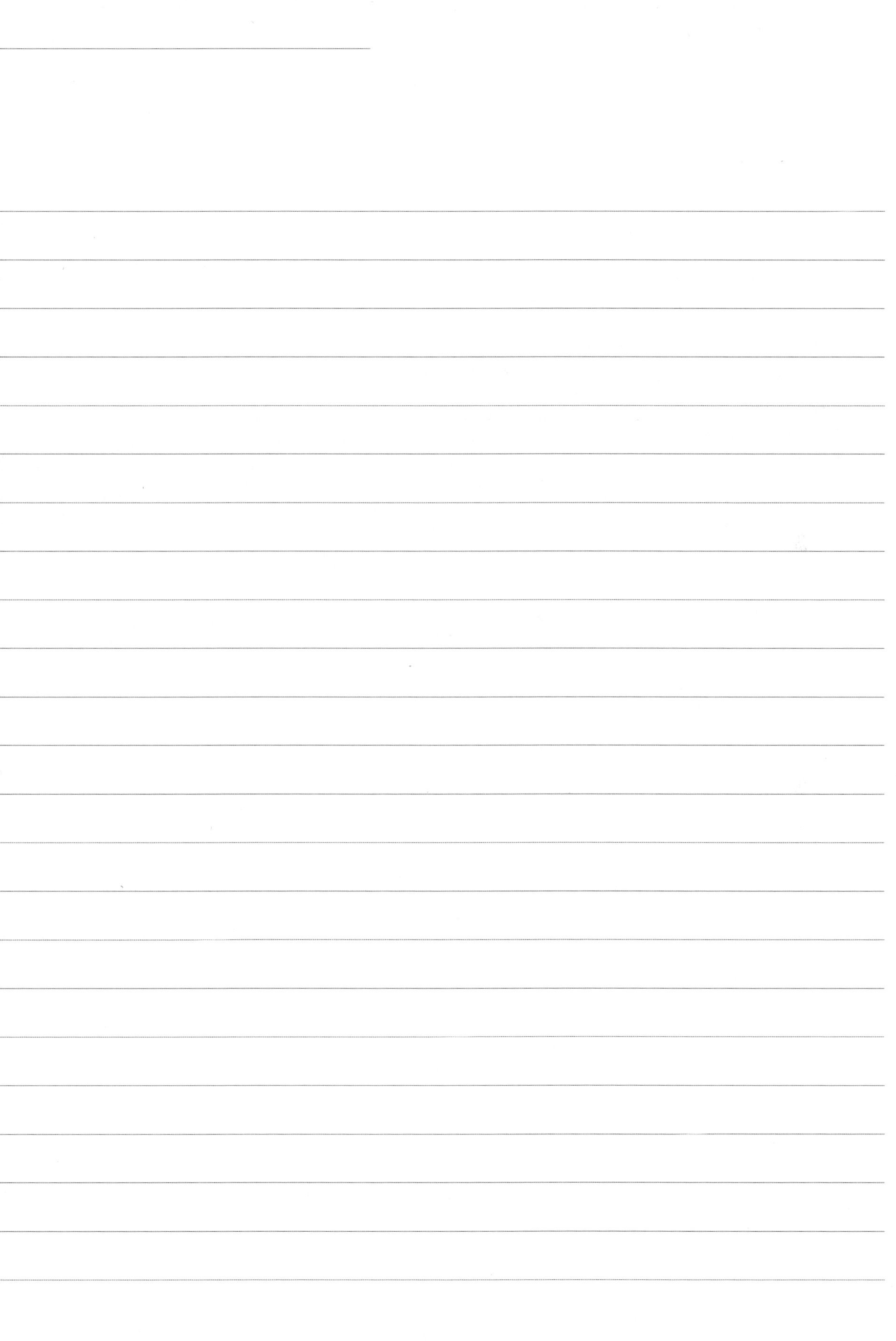

Made in the USA
Monee, IL
07 July 2026

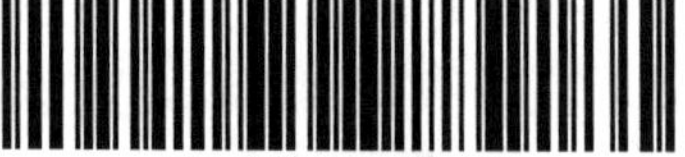

56551528R00061